OPIUM AND AMBERGRIS

Wick Poetry First Book Series

DAVID HASSLER, EDITOR

The Local World by Mira Rosenthal	Maggie Anderson, Judge
Wet by Carolyn Creedon	Edward Hirsch, Judge
The Dead Eat Everything by Michael Mlekoday	Dorianne Laux, Judge
The Spectral Wilderness by Oliver Bendorf	Mark Doty, Judge
Translation by Matthew Minicucci	Jane Hirshfield, Judge
hover over her by Leah Poole Osowski	Adrian Matejka, Judge
Even Years by Christine Gosnay	Angie Estes, Judge
Fugue Figure by Michael McKee Green	Khaled Mattawa, Judge
The Many Names for Mother by Julia Kolchinsky Dasbach	Ellen Bass, Judge
On This Side of the Desert by Alfredo Aguilar	Natalie Diaz, Judge
How Blood Works by Ellene Glenn Moore	Richard Blanco, Judge
Sister Tongue زبان خواهر by Farnaz Fatemi	Tracy K. Smith, Judge
Fraternal Light: On Painting While Black by Arlene Keizer	Cornelius Eady, Judge
Opium and Ambergris by Colin Dekeersgieter	Marilyn Chin, Judge

MAGGIE ANDERSON, EDITOR EMERITA

Already the World by Victoria Redel	Gerald Stern, Judge
Likely by Lisa Coffman	Alicia Suskin Ostriker, Judge
Intended Place by Rosemary Willey	Yusef Komunyakaa, Judge
The Apprentice of Fever by Richard Tayson	Marilyn Hacker, Judge
Beyond the Velvet Curtain by Karen Kovacik	Henry Taylor, Judge
The Gospel of Barbecue by Honorée Fanonne Jeffers	Lucille Clifton, Judge
Paper Cathedrals by Morri Creech	Li-Young Lee, Judge
Back Through Interruption by Kate Northrop	Lynn Emanuel, Judge
The Drowned Girl by Eve Alexandra	C. K. Williams, Judge
Rooms and Fields: Dramatic Monologues from the War in Bosnia by Lee Peterson	Jean Valentine, Judge
Trying to Speak by Anele Rubin	Philip Levine, Judge
Intaglio by Ariana-Sophia M. Kartsonis	Eleanor Wilner, Judge
Constituents of Matter by Anna Leahy	Alberto Rios, Judge
Far from Algiers by Djelloul Marbrook	Toi Derricotte, Judge
The Infirmary by Edward Micus	Stephen Dunn, Judge
Visible Heavens by Joanna Solfrian	Naomi Shihab Nye, Judge

Opium and Ambergris

Poems by

Colin Dekeersgieter

The Kent State University Press

Kent, Ohio

ISBN 978-1-60635-483-4
Manufactured in the United States of America

The Wick Poetry Series is sponsored by the Stan and Tom Wick Poetry Center and the Department of English at Kent State University.

Cataloging information for this title is available at the Library of Congress.

28 27 26 25 24   5 4 3 2 1

for my Brother
through my Mother

for my Mother
through my Brother

CONTENTS

Almost every poem in *Opium and Ambergris* unapologetically spotlights the themes of addiction and mental illness. An unbearable grief unsettles us through multiple vignettes of overdoses, psyche wards, suicide attempts, and failing relationships. Colin Dekeersgieter's book is a visceral and immersive experience, with lines that linger in the mind long after reading.

One of my favorite poems is the title work, "Opium and Ambergris." The poem is a brilliant fretwork of incongruous motifs. Ambergris is a waxy substance produced in the digestive system of sperm whales. It was highly valued in the nineteenth century for the making of medical elixirs and is still used today in some perfumes. Commercial greed caused the whale to be hunted almost to extinction. We see a similar extinction happening in the pages of this book. In "Opium and Ambergris," I appreciate the mother, who is intimately entwined with her addicted son, devoted but complicitous in his dying, cleaning after his mess, but with ambivalence:

> She hates to love
> that at least he's here, quiet as a whale
>
> dying under water. She lights a WoodWick candle;
> it spits and she tears up. Blood runs down his arm
> from a punctured blot and forms
> a dainty cross in the folds of an inactive wrist.
> Is it too soon, she thinks, to turn to Christ?

The poet juxtaposes heavy symbols with surprising off-beat motifs, mixing the sacred with the profane: whale against human; heroin against ambergris; the aroma of Chanel perfume against the stench of death; the blood of Christ against the blood of the addict.

The best poems exhibit both Stevens's grace and Plath's dark energy, with which Dekeersgieter makes self-destruction shine with gorgeous ease. Metaphors like substances abound. And paraphernalia permeates our senses: warped syringes, cooked spoons, grapes painted with Demerol, "seepage glitter." The poem "Mementos" teases our ears with this materialism through gruesome tongue twisters and cacophony:

before the bodies were worn
by an opal drink's finicky taste
or an oval bevel on a warped needle
sipping poppy's silic sap
from pewter spoons for flawless hits
in minute hollows of the neck;

I admire Dekeersgieter's playful exploration of sound here as well as his
formal and stylistic variations throughout. He is eager to try different
modes: sonnets, formalized triplet sequences, sestinas, aubades, couplets,
full- and off-rhymed stanzas, and poems that drift in a compositional
field. In "Immolation," the poet uses airy, sardonic rhyming that floats
in fragmented quatrains:

Your face comes to mind   as my hand burns.
Sheets of me wilt on the pan   like saran.
    What a gas.   What a scent I am.
        Such a scene.

This play is coupled with work that explores deep emotional pain, em-
bodying a lyric voice that is personal, familial, and universal. Throughout
Dekeersgieter's sonic play and formal experimentation, there are mo-
ments of heartfelt illumination and confessional one-liners: "I need life
to speak to me the manner in which suspense is the answer."

We are held in this suspense throughout the work as Dekeersgieter
refuses to let us look away from his central theme: addiction is an urgent,
intransigent problem and may ultimately destroy the American family.
Opium and Ambergris is a fascinating first book, and we look forward
to relishing more work from this poet.

ACKNOWLEDGMENTS

This book began in solitude and ended in community. I am grateful for the words, eyes, and ears of the friends, family, and writers who have shaped and reshaped these poems in profound ways. It would be difficult to name everyone, but I would like to expressly thank the following people:

The editors of the journals in which several poems in this collection, sometimes earlier versions of them, originally appeared: *Brink*: "Antigone" and "Swift Symbiosis." *Green Mountains Review*: "Visitation." *Grey Sparrow Journal*: "Still Life with Grapes and a Swift." *North American Review*: "A Hand's Breadth" and "Contacts." *The Greensboro Review*: "Saturn in Sagittarius." *The Paris-American*: "Magnificat." *The Worcester Review*: "The Anthologists."

Marilyn Chin, not only for seeing the merit in this work but for her spirit in the world of poetry.

Everyone at the Wick Poetry Center; Wick Poetry Center director David Hassler, for his attention to my manuscript, especially as it shifted in the final stages. The team at the Kent State University Press, including Susan Wadsworth-Booth, Mary Young, Chris Brooks, Julia Wiesenberg, and the many others who brought the book to print.

Everyone at the New York University Creative Writing Program. Diannely Antiqua, Dominique Bechard, Ama Codjoe, Laura Cresté, Linda Dolan, Ethan Fortuna, Yael Hacohen, Alisha Kaplan, George Kovalenko, Yuxi Lin, Rachel Mannheimer, M'Bilia Meekers, Maggie Millner, Holly Mitchell, Jessica Modi, Vanessa Moody, Maddie Mori, Mallory Imler Powell, Lindsey Skillen, Eleanor Wright, Jihyun Yun, and the many friends and workshop peers at NYU whose attention, insight, and writing continue to impact my work. Thank you for your language and laughter in the classroom and through the evenings.

My incredible teachers over the years: Ed Hirsch, Major Jackson, Wayne Koestenbaum, Catherine Barnett, Sharon Olds, Matthew Rohrer, Yusef Komunyakaa, Meghan O'Rourke, and Anne Carson, your support and inspiration remain invaluable.

Leo Collins, uncle Leo, thank you for being a part of our family. Dustin Baker, Will Clavelle, Robbie Elsman, Ben Green, Jason Murray, Jake O'Brien, Derek Stubbs, Evan Watson, your love and friendship has sustained me my entire life. Thank you for keeping me alive. Francisco Márquez, your intelligence and humor has consistently bettered me and my labors in this vocation. Kylan Rice, we have thankfully been "Too strange to each other for misunderstanding." Your words, vision, and way of being push me in untold ways. Alexandria Hall, you taught me to read me and remain my confidante in emotional and literary emergency. To all of you, your friendship, style, and teachings are in this book.

My sister Caitlin. These poems are *for* you more than they're for anyone else; you sit in my conscience and drive any empathy I may have. My father Robert, who has taught me to do right and to never stop doing. My mother Margery, my first reader and my *OED*. You deserve more than this. Alisa Koyrakh, my wife, my best friend and reader. You gave me the only knowledge of love that could work these poems through the dark. Zora Inna Dekeersgieter, my ε, I love you this much ·

OPIUM AND AMBERGRIS

My mother spins into a spritz of Chanel N°5
as my brother boils his spit in a spoon to nod
off and on and on along to *Hunky Dory,* endlessly
affirming the worst: the rot has gotten in the blood.
She cleans and hums his Bowie back,
spirited by a caustic mix of vinegar and lime
to mask the fragrance—clear as iodine—
that's settled in the walls. She hates to love
that at least he's here, quiet as a whale

dying under water. She lights a WoodWick candle;
it spits and she tears up. Blood runs down his arm
from a punctured blot and forms
a dainty cross in the folds of an inactive wrist.
Is it too soon, she thinks, to turn to Christ?
She fears this fiercest quiet she will miss
and rushes floors with lemoned mops, mouthing
A crack in the sky and a hand reaching down
to me . . . She wrings his blood out in the sink.

I. OPIUM

The frown like serpents basking on the brow,
The spent feeling leaving nothing of itself . . .
— *Wallace Stevens*

MEMENTOS

i.

Before *phenobarbital* was a word
rare as *molasses,* not *never* used, not *not* sweet,
I was telling baubles opal notions
hoping to jealous trifles into totems,
to relic trinkets amulets.
They only ever answered with ellipses,
spinning three bores into their own filigree.
Even my inanimates
hurt themselves and leave
that same mineral perfume my relatives leave
in urns on respective credenzas
|Boiled Spit|Fresh Fell|Copper Bloom|

ii.

Before good brains and solid hearts
began to boil in juniper foam;
before the bodies were worn
by an opal drink's finicky taste
or an oval bevel on a warped needle
sipping poppy's silic sap
from pewter spoons for flawless hits
in minute hollows of the neck;
I placed each deathly expectation
between pages, blue-veined petals
pressed and taxonomized
|Base|Tallow|Inhalant|Snuff|

iii.

Each dim inscription invariably reads:
From complications with [ellipsis].
My mother's mother fits inside
a gewgaw and her father looks

like sand. My brother danced his dance
of damage well, then died alone
in Maine, brain-bruised and opiated.
He relearned to walk and swallow water.
He relearned how to think and talk
about his brother's future daughter.
Now he's |After Ember|Charcoal|
and fits in a rig box beside John-Michael.

Name three things you see.

Electrodes being brought just to her temple.
Electrodes and a kiss on my temple.
My twelve meridians are charged of her
and I see in her voice and repetitions
that hers are charged of her and nothing else.
I see that she is charged of one of her past selves
and nothing else, no one but her Who I Was.

Name three things you see.

Through the square pane
of the secured door
on the ER's psych ward
I register the difference in our heights and feel big and above her
for the first time.

I collect myself as her child more dearly
than a day ago and say "Yes, I see
the gown is stained," and "Sorry,
I don't see the concern
with being unclean."

Name three things you see.

Perhaps glass. The brink of a road. Everything supine.

Name three things you hear.

A candid wind.
The labored breath of children.
    My mother mouthing
    "What is happening?" once more
    through a fastened door.
This whole continuum thing isn't working.

Yesterday we were catapults
and now
I'd like to rest a while.

Name three things you hear.

Wind on the brink.
Breathing on the brink.
  Everything supine.
Laughter in the nurses' station.

Name three things you feel.

I feel my being
held by ligaments—that I am of a piece.
I feel the intricacies of my spine and I sweat.
  I'd like to put my life back
  into pieces beside hers.
  We don't want to be whole.
  In the ward she believes more
  immediately than in the world
  that one should be complete.

  But she's convinced a sentence split her
  person along several meridians.
  She's convinced a line changed
  her life and I say "That's impossible"
  with no heart to tell her
  a line changes my life every day.

Name three things you feel.

I feel the electrodes being brought to her just temple.
I feel her kiss on my temple.
  I feel the alacrity of anger.
  I feel across me for my child in the sleepless evenings.

I feel a prescience for tomorrow,
which is the disease: the lack
of compassion for her Who She Is,
the hurt of her promise to work gone fallow
again; the repetition, the "Was I good?"
I feel a need for a brink, the blank,
some terminus, my Lord
I feel undeserving
of this pain.
God I've been good.

VISITATION

What strengthened me, for you was lethal.
—Czesław Miłosz

I was never bent on saving you.
It meant a coddling kind of language:
I hear you. You're seen.
Anyhow, I couldn't stop drinking
long enough to seem credible.

I don't regret a thing.

Spinoza said that if triangles could speak
they would have triangular gods.
So my speech could only deify you,
you who were normal
as the sky is normal—I mean
you hung around all unexplained,
with an imperceptible weightiness
and a good smile.
And from the beginning
your stature was my salvation:
it took my eyes to certain heights
until I noticed pennants spires birds
and all the other poems floating beside your head.

If I said a word, I'd chase you both off,
poem and person, because poetry is a body
embodying a hope
faint as the edges
of a shadow being lit;
and your body had always been
a fragile gadget, living
by being among the shadows that it lights.

You and poetry have scared me
into becoming a person
less honest than these exaggerations.

Any moment, Apollo will cut my throat.

Like an old derrick trammeled to its shore
Brennan was bent on affirming his utility
in a town where many ships had sailed home
only to be lost to winches weakened
by currents, exhausted by commerce: rolled
smoke above the invasive alders, stonecutter
dust limning dogwood and dutchman's pipe
in lime, mule hooves beating haloes in dirt.
But he was cut for thought and exhausting
confidence tricks. He took up Zoroaster, learned
sales quips, flipped Audis, leaked sayings like
*pennies on the dollar, move the needle, a shot
in the arm, hit bottom line,* move the needle

into the thigh all the while wishing for mansions,
new swag, and no body: a Beamer and oblivion.
Because he did think *Why these trappings
at all? Why this guile of bodies of laws?
Laws provided to hinder, to test our constitution
then dose our constitution to fix our constitution
then judge us all asunder for our new fixations?*
as he tore quiet squares from *The Gay Science*
and a facsimile of Durer's *Melancholia I*
and rolled them into neat piping to bang Oxy,
inhaling smithereens of hourglass and angel
robe, watching bright, waxen dashes of blood
leak from the nose and redact all sentiment:

"there is nothing mor ████████████████
"Beside you is the ocean:" freedom seethed for him
in foam and distance formed of a glassine gray
and running out to glassy edge where deleterious
tides gestured Saturn through a deleterious moon
promising cycles of quick, quiet, and complete
economics welling to spill in delectation or ripple
away with discontentment. Because he did think

*Why bisect, apportion land and sanity, claim
lunatics and seas (but only up to a point), defy
coherence, belie it, give, sanction, rescind, repeal,
drive all dog-tired until the 201-mile-long drift
to international waters seems a breeze, a boon?*

INTRUSIVE THOUGHTS

It's taken thirty years
botching tomatoes
to know how keenly an edge slips through

    —wooden coffin shut
    hair stuck
    —shock-kick of a nail gun shot
       gone   *Ah*
    shut in a body
       staid as moral Seneca

.

I'm learning to get my sister to speak with me.
I'm learning the give of avocado meat.
Put almost no pressure on the hilt

    —bladeglint   throat
    peach trickle
    —to whom?
      Agenbite of inwit
    sister father animal
      Yet here's—Gone—Ah

.

This is how you crack the egg for eating.
This is the tone to use when speaking.
This is how you get honey from the queen:

a slight concavity in the hand, as if receiving
the giving of a coin, as if doling out a peach
as gently as placing a bead in a dimple's bed

    —then a needle through the cheek—

.

ANACHRONISTS

He frisked the morning for its clarity
as an overdose, goodly and measured,
floated about his eye and reek.
I had my someteenth drink
in the partlight, in the dark mirror
like, *Some teeth.*
           I wanted cognac
for lunch. I wanted a sidecar.
I wanted to drag you through earth
gnawing the numbing root.
How will we shirk barbarity?

         We were our own banes
for two decades, skewed
in the prudence of a wrong century.
Our sex, our hair, our clothes, it was all inapt.
You could have let me coif that grassy mop
with pomade. Let me call those quaffs
         Aspirin and Dinner.
Into which boot did I slip
that switchblade? When we finally looked,
the sun was running late.
We poured libations on the light.

MAGNIFICAT

and there's an intimation of birth
in the rain the house lets in.

    But everyone calls us poor.

If they bring it up again
tell them we're phy-sis-a-philes.
Where's your brother? That wild—

    He's in the flowerbed with a magnifying glass
    learning of the aphid and the cabbage maggot
    trying not to burn any calyx stalk or bine
    with his exacting science
    of distance and still hands.
    He's the garden
    and the tremulous map.
    There's an X marked with treasure
    and he's trailing a blaze
    bridging the burn
    and frenzy feeding.
    It's Magnificat! His soul
    magnifies mom. He will be
    contrapassoed glorious
    imagine
    metempsychosised firefly.

That's the way he lived

    and sinned with the light of his eyes
    going greenly bright and black
    greenly black and bright
    at the sea with the earth at his back.

Does he think that we can house him here?
That we can make our house his home
despite the holes?

There is an intimation . . .

    He believes he can live off rationed rain
    eat our papers and suck the pulp
    out of the wood

As if Adam hadn't swerved

    as if
    there would be a shadow at the door.

There would be a shadow at the door.

HOW TO STAND BESIDE YOUR MOTHER
WHEN SHE SETS YOUR HOME ON FIRE

As the snow makes the night shine
    piecemeal, and the shine makes the salt
shine too, tug her cuff, ask if it's happened.

    Pretend to be distracted by her voice
and not the mirror wind makes of her voice
    filled with was and maybe this maybe that

docile Chagall isn't bleeding colors
    of possession fleet as firs. Her hand
will find your hand and it will burn

    hot with the puppy left to the storm in '94.
Do not let your brain mention its body,
    its budding fur clogging the sewers.

Ask, where is the new dog, flammable
    as a sock and afraid to whine?
Don't ask at what temperature dog melts.

    When prayer finds you, let it have you.
Speak to it. Speak to her. Tell her
    you've never felt this warm.

EMBODIMENT

we put his ash in desert fire
now his ashed teeth & hair
fire's a body blood & bone
so his body burned my hand
& with an animating transfer
it hissed a dry Adamic word
I held light death to the light
until the exposure brightened

scorched by desert wind
his ashed skin is ash trifold
embodied in a fire is a body
his hand burned my hand
my hand shook his death alive
putting my hand near fire again
& let ash sieve from my hand
burned brightened then hurt

that night I saw a desert fox
the only thing alive was fox
the fox flashed fire all night
in the morning a warm dent
a snug Q of a huddled being

all low ashen slick & sharp
& an ember's last hop in ash
licking at spat pith & bones
was sunk softly in the sand
beside my still burning hand

A HAND'S BREADTH

When I hear the voice that woke me with a hand over my mouth,
humming "Psycho Suite" or "The Imperial March," my throat closes up

and I have to rush off the thought of one last tolerant god to relearn
the physics of swallowing *I love myself I love myself I love myself*

though I've done nothing to ease the world. As a child, the voice
tried to balance out the earth, bringing soil from the garden

to the island's roots loosed in the fast panache of a hurricane.
Still, it laughed more than it cried. We laughed more than we fought

but not by much, which doesn't mean much. When I confessed
I killed the man-o-war and the voice asked if it had a face, I only said

No because I was thinking of its hands (I've always looked to hands).
I only saw what I still see: its rotund plea, its pleated crest

like a bloated sailfish with its dorsal fin array all astray, bereft
of any will to lollygag or dash or bat its placeless eyes

as I wrecked its passive bladder and listened to its pneuma seep.
I want to see the world and all its seepage glitter thick like tar.

I want to open wounds the aperture of stars in snails and oak
with salts and picks to see the strongest things contract and pulp.

I want to push a whale's face into the sand. We had such similar hands.
On the gurney, I note the breadth of purple beneath the muted teeth.

I love myself I love myself and *He loved me* and *He loved me.*
The last time I saw him, the earth was beneath his fingernails.

THE CONDITION OF ALONE

We all went into the room, one by one.
Scars like eskers on a solid lemon,
avocado-soft and treated with staples
up the abdomen and over the blue breast,
woke me. The older blue, bluing of punctures
with staid blood sunk, staying, Opheliac
and cold and content to relinquish a hold on complexion
woke me. The older, lonelier, bluer death.

And now my wife's mother-in-law has gone
and gone all blue too, with a pill-stopped heart
jumped by an ex with Narcan. Staggering,
history's going. The only difference a
variance in the condition of "alone," for which
there's no definition, only a sliding scale.

.Transpose armor   into sword   ,sword into foil
.The counter nimble

                         ,pinned   to the abdomen

          .Night shifts   calm to translucence
and the riled
                swift   is dutiful

as flame   .Then
        the swift wound
                    to all care   transfixes heraldry

;the queen melts   to ruin
        ,the kingdom
                    melts   into bluestone ruin

          .Things that flash   like armor now   ,like swords
in service

                         ,they're just   birds

The Boy Eater keeps his voice
like mercury. It doesn't hark
to the chasm but culls
with coos to the gutter.
In the event of my drowning,
don't disinter my bloated body.
When I'm bittered to bone
I'll give my ribcage back to mothers
and their young. Let me be a substrate
for gravid sharks to latch an egg case on.
I'll hold a brother into this world
and not out. There is time.
Time to reap more mermaid purse and leek.
Time for me to prove I'm a centaur.
Maybe I only have preternatural aim.
So what that I can swim and climb?
So what that I'm ruled by the legs?
Remember sitting.
Remember when trauma was only a coma
in the soaps. Remember feeding Saturn
the eyes of Ops
and forming her little sharks
into blind fish so they couldn't see
the black cavity in father's molar?
When I find the Hunger that killed you,
I will bend back my bow, and I will breathe.
I will ask to see the contents of its stomach.

You should've heard my tone when father gave me over
to the police
—Is this—Is my mother dead?
calm as the season.
I didn't rush to your death, doing my all
to not be like you.

The officer said you were going
to the State Hospital, and was I
headed there?
I wasn't, but I was
going somewhere.
I was going to get you back.

I turned and turned,
hoping to never turn again.
There was no music on in the car, that felt noble,
despite my awareness of almost lollygagging
to your deathfloor.

And that's where you were,
all feet
framed in a door, and I thought
Pretty poor resuscitation.

Answering questions. Making up answers.
Giving the wrong address out of confusion
or a shared, osmotic disdain for cops,
and particularly this one's wide, lambkin eyes
and good stubble. He asked
How do you spell "Hy-drox-y-zine?"
Like it sounds lambkin,
nothing said.

That's the system that lost you, naturally.
No one under that name arrived
at this State Hospital.

No
Jane Doe in the morgue.
No no
Jane Doe in the morgue.

Hours later, on a hill very near,
the police and the EMS with all their designs
in their white, dimpled mouths,
tossed their heads in sprightly dance
and watched the potential of a woman
recently dead
walk off with nothing
but a will to die.

She refused treatment.

Sockless in a Paris Green gown
I encountered you with no shock and a wire
hitched to somewhere swung to your shins.

Going somewhere?

And asking that in that way
and seeing you with your wide disquieted eyes and your head
lifted and cocked as if determined
to never look into the canyon from your practiced wire,
I thought I might split your murderous pill.

From somewhere, father.

We urged you to the slow sliding doors
and your dissolution gathered its intelligence:

                    I am here of my own volition,
                         something said.

IMMOLATION

Your face comes to mind   as my hand burns.
Sheets of me wilt on the pan   like saran.
       What a gas.   What a scent I am.
             Such a scene.

I've smelled myself   burning before,
selves kindle   sure as nothing goes
       wingfirst   into fire. The real trouble
         is with the honey of sight,

how it sticks to everything: flesh bubbles,
touched velour,   fireweed,
       neon,   read receipts
         from the too-long dead.

One must convince oneself   to doubt
an ellipsis   means anything.
       I want to collapse   our apsides
         to touch the central body

fixing this distance.   I want us to look like Mars
and sip nectar.   I want to ferment
       picked asphodel   and binge
         until cicadas dip down

to snicker near the gloaming   of our pores.
I'm big tonight with aura: I feel a little flambeau.
       My hair is going.   What a gas.
         What a wretch I am.

Scandent carnations   sting into bloom
up the flippancy of skin.   I imagine out
       -leaping   this planar scheme
         to touch my vision to your cheek

when the eyes,   slowest to go
as flames reach face meat   late,
        greet your ghost   like a cleaver meets bone
            clothed in briar and smoke.

Then suddenly   I'm healed. Or
I'm hurt but   never better.
        Life took the brunt   of the burning,
            my sight's pristine as ever.

THE CHEF AND THE WREN

He admires a mote of all-purpose
flour upon his love line.

The city is half-given
in a lambent sonogram of snow.
Seen in a systole drift
is a single wren
with an auburn crown
and a taupe belly sloped
below its freckled wings
freckled taupe.

Bird, he asks, what is North?

a a peak   drilled deep in me
through genes   the deep-seat
to to
a bird who jigs in heat
to woo
so as to cool
what's cooped in me

to renew   anew wren's brood
pursue food   pursue
refuge
move move pursue pursue
to hop
to hop aside
from life and die

The chef's rapt to the spangle
of a similar music. Ditties
sibylline as snowfall convince him
he too is affixed
to an eagerness for issue.

There is no more
the hand of fire can gather
to teach him life's will to wonderment
in a time whose every speech is juncture,
every half-trilled twitter
an urgent stutter, cataclysms
written with snow on water.

He sees a mote of purpose
light upon his love line
and knows there is a calm
at the end of the mind
in which a bird
who only sings to birds resides.

NECROMANCY

I asked wildflowers your whereabouts and sunk
your shirts into oceans to see if you'd take form
and drown. Then I burned Ovid in spite—
only to see your nose: it was of smoke
dissembled in its own smoke.

Like when I found you years ago,
smokey eye lash line to brow bone with a lit match
to hush-hush liner. You lashed out against me
when I hoped we might pleasure in accentuation
a touch-up more. Now I love you with a love

mute as the foundation stippled in your pores.
I'm not sorry for considering your contours
or how some blush could shape our fates.
This nuanced knowledge of your tricky skin
helps me conjure up your perfect shade.

TRUCE

The sky was gray above the banyans.
Brennan, late to truce, stood with his head
tipped upward, bleeding from the nose.
And Kiki with a nip from a snake on his ankle
asked if we saw it. What was its pattern?

I made a dance the pattern
and was appropriately ignored,
having won.

I noted the sky's changing light
and how the clouds passed
more quickly than the shade they cast.
I made the comments
I was taught to lean forward
when bleeding from the nose
and to find the snake
and kiss it. I was ignored,
having won.

The banyans walked into the water.

In that blackening truce I opened up
a lore along myself (being too anxious
for plot and too damaged for myth).
I learned just how criminal I could really get,
how much I could hurt everything.

I wanted to rename me.

    Maybe I did

as the inbreaking clouds
folded on themselves unseemly but adorning
and rolled in me like that very night,
of which I wasn't afraid.
I was getting big.
It was getting darker.

SWIFT HISTORY

We are the creatures of a gone country, gone.
The palisades gone, the arcades, the blue marlins, gone.

You do, though, this countrifying thing.
You be and do and stand on the stair like a palinode,

like a swift leaving its plumb perchance, but you stand.
It was here, the country, before we arrived. I assume

you know that. And this revolution too has had its moment
and put you out like a Madonna, like an Ugolino, sans progeny.

II. AMBERGRIS

Now that the incorruption of this most fragrant ambergris
should be found in the heart of such decay; is this nothing?
—*Herman Melville*

SWIFT SYMBIOSIS

Pray the house triumph   tugging the cornerstone

It has to do with wanting   to escape
the failures of my lineage
I want to do right   not swift
I need life to speak to me the manner in which suspense is the answer
the way that being without being withheld being suspended
is what's up

Don't you know I will kill   for this and them
Don't you think the constant actual and peripheral loss is enough
to mention   or blurt
the dead brother
and the mother killing herself
while all the while
threatening to kill herself   Don't you think that that's enough

    I move some distance from the sun to find more sun

The cataclysms are nothing   more than lichen in the trees
a slow burgeoning for springtails to engulf
as slow as the burgeoning   That's life now

eating what's growing   slow enough so you can live and it can live
to grow and slow your growing demise

For instance   I hear this whirring
belonging to no one   and call it ocean
It eats my eardrum near to ruin and I thank it
being deeply inland   Though I'm losing certain tones
in my child's voice   I can hum the ocean back to her

Whatever it is you hear or touch or ask to know
How can we embed   that is what is killing you

Learn it   taste it   attenuate it
remain alive

APUS APUS IN AIR

Stony the night goes
suspended.
Stony the ocean draped.
The world suspended.
The things of the world suspended
and all small and great, all stone and drape
equally upended.

        The swift runs the sea's length.

I aim to run contented home
and hunt contentment long from estuary to esker;
aim to flush it and prevent its having treed;
aim to sift it from dew-grass; to rout it out
from Bimini Road to bridge; to do the work;
to self-estimate in this profane topsy
violated, decimated,
loved, and having done;
loved a love suspended,
a love overpassed to,
through them, through salt, through this dis
-contended world risen
and dropped, earth-lost, asea in air;
      then the Line
got to, overpassed, so never
alone on a wide wide sea
and linking new inroads into
this predilection to air love.

AUBADE

From too many pockets morning pulls
light like a father home for the day.
I think on all I imagine I'll need:

keys, tender, sabbaths, and space.
I think of raising a child as a litmus test
for love and touch my mouth back

to my wife's just temple, fall mostly to sleep,
see myself walking through many cuts
in different forests into new clearings

I hardly remember in memorable countries.
Spire intimations of a worn-out culture—
then the impression of a frog's or bird's

dulcet ounces on top of bone-dry duff.
It smarts to know this: taste is just mineral
lighting on the tongue. Warm the tinged flavors

of air between our chests and call them
This, Is, and Certain. I'm as sad as the earth.
I'm poor in a good way. I'm where I want to be.

Are these sound delusions my way of prayer?
Asking alone might be the revelation, but
it is impossible to tell us anything. The animal

and the mineral world go on changing, but
boy I like her. And everything I know of frogs
is likely a lie, like words are better than skin.

Life lives like warm creatures near her ear;
the earth in me wakes and forms. This is
certain: together, our chests breathe in.

EXTRINSIC FORCES

          Between my daughter's homecoming
and my respite I received word from my senescent mother:
"Colonizers can't take this anymore."
It's a late realization, she in her dotage, presumed
trapped in her age with its denials of history.
"They should go back to their fraught provinces,"
I wanted to write, to jeer her desperate ego and its fingers
and point out the irony of her digital slip of the tongue:
a covert realization that she's been set upon
by extrinsic forces. Spotting a hawk in its vesture
mounted above the marsh's matins, aloof as a leper,
I leaped, thinking, *Go awing, give grace, sturdy thing!*
I didn't intrude.

          I once plucked a common nighthawk
from its acreage with the grille of a high-beaming rental
north of the Mojave. Pulling it out, safe from renown disease
with thin, plastic gas-up gloves, it nearly tore.
I learned its genus by the white blazes on the wrists
of its wings: Chordeiles, night dancer, the booming bullbat.
Not sturdy at all, hardly even solid. I felt sick
from its paltry weight and my incessant encroachment
on others' lives.

          "Colonizers," I know,
having interpreted her dashed rhetoric for years, is
"Colin, I just" can't take this anymore. "This" being
depression, the colonizer, which entered through our teeth.
The colonizers are dead but their organisms are
in our soil, leaching into our water and, once in the blood,
generate a poison.

          Soon I'll pull my mother up once more
from the floor of whatever newest lacuna she's colonized.
She'll come away from it like tangled sprouts,
ingathered but not firmly fixed, and there may be apologies

through the apophatic calm on her face. We won't discuss
the incessant trauma of this interloping disease. I won't say,
What on earth now.

STILL LIFE WITH GRAPES AND A SWIFT

Zeuxis, who represented some grapes, painted so naturally
that the birds flew towards the spot where the painting was exhibited.
    —Pliny the Elder

This is that art which can veil without will
the imprimatura, the first whisht, the swiftbird
tucked of wing, dropping or rising through
this fallen forest, tucking its tone into morning.
This is after the cutting, stretching, tacking linen
to the board, after the starlings elicited vineyards
on the hill. Below the hill, the stones will be cold
as the measured swish of decerebrated tadpoles,
ignoring algae wafers that mushroom in the scum.
We are babyfrogs, reft of want, wanting something
like a sacrum, a vesica piscis, some sort of nimbus,
some impetus. But we're busy with indifference.
One must cut out so much—sugar   silk   acids—
to feel the fizz of dopamine in the grass, its element
of cat tongue. Those abrasions are worth living for.
Wild grapes that look fatal, as if they were painted
with Demerol, are worth living for. There's something
to admire there before the taste. There was something
there before taste and the knowledge of them tasting.
There should be a reintroduction to this, a meeting
of minds arranged with the palimpsest. With the swift
we dip for tinted grapes. It's all mimicry at a distance.

RECENT HISTORY SESTINA

In March we went wild to do our nails.
Picking colors, all agreed you've good taste.
Over humming bubbles you said you'd work
hard to forgive misgivings of your past
and start to wean off the clonazepam.
My daughter turned her body, turned a wheel.

You said, Once, history was like a wheel,
not something involving a bat and nails.
Now that you're weaning off clonazepam
you say in general you've lost your taste
for bitter Buddhists rehashing the past.
You did it for years and it didn't work.

"Keep coming back it works if you work
it." I suggested a kind of chore wheel
to randomize a system of getting past
addictive trauma. I needed wood, nails.
But you hadn't exactly lost your taste
for the chaste and bittern clonazepam

and we all wondered, Why clonazepam?
What does it do to the brain? How does it work?
Used for seizures, panic; impairs judgment, taste.
Oma had seizures. Three grand mals at the wheel.
I thought you'd be keen to incoming nails
in the coffin, obsessed with ghosts going past.

In May you say you've only had a past.
So then it's always been clonazepam.
Maybe, no matter how many firm nails
on the chalkboard, you never did the work,
never looked at the slope and then the wheel
and pushed up, paused, pushed up beyond the taste

of common, solemn loss; beyond the taste
of your hateful predilection for the past.
I could give in and let the whole thing wheel
into Fentanyl and clonazepam;
wheeling it back to your first son might work.
That wasn't suicide, right? Earth in his nails

and so on. No one has a taste for the past.
Clonazepam, talk, ECT, it's all work.
If you spin the wheel, I'll pry the nails.

THE GRAVITY OF GRACE

If the sky is clear and we're not found
wanting, not mulling over what we've done
to bugs, but rather thinking
or feigning to think of the success
of winter water lilies—and now
a ring, now a child, full stop—
then that's the scope of evening
despite the mass of content,
the elliptic of form, the orbit
of rearing: this damage near, that far,

linked through hesitation.

We daub blood off the palms
of our child with an unwashed towel.
A strange monogram abrades her skin.
But as by grace fire aspires to air
though it can be done in by dirt,
she reaches upward from her toes and
upward from her toes and upward
from her toes. Three kisses.
The lilies begin to close. We will
secure the casements before she's cold.

SWIFT SESSION

I gather the stones from my child's mouth
in the roundabout at the Adult Psychiatry Clinic
and build a cairn up the face of a curb.
The sapling announces itself to spring.

Hyacinths bloom spike bloom
and lean
under echoes of the nearly passerine.

> *Keep me in grace.*
> *Keep me from leveling.*

She spits stones from her mouth. I gather them in a neat pile.
I don't consider that my mother is dying or the type of death

it is becoming.

The stones.
The sapling.

The inflorescence ingathers
as the hyacinths spikebloom and lean into spring
shadows not their own
under the passersby.

I guess it's a dogwood flung well and seeded
with all that intelligence through its very unhollow.

With an empty mouth
my child imitates the noonish whistlings.
This is how we pass the time.
The sapling, the swifts, the wet stones.

> *Keep me skewed*
> *in grace.*

Sessions are an hour.

ARS POETICA

Nothing sidles in the summer like hawk moths
along the margins of the yard. Nothing knows a why
like abjured pith, perishment, and spiderspit in swath.
I find I'm for the fauna fading with the whistles
in the verdigris. So I match my body to the mourning
cloak butterfly and I speckle down my orderly border.
I get like paper, but less. I cleave. And once cleft
I light upon my sacrum without heft to tap out type
with a lepidopteran ditty in my head called, *To Slug,
From Incompetence, with Love*—so named for nothing
could touch the decency of a leopard-blotched mollusc.
No prose or skyward ode could ape its glister on the world.

        I think of my own unseemly coat as I watch ants wander
      with their mandibles in birdrot, feet stuck in a finch's guts
          or the bubbled spume of a sparrow. Is it any wonder
            I mix whole husk psyllium with whiskey and water
        when every inch of me is pouring out of me for June?
             The song is gone. And the slug. Its wake desiccates
        on rotting wood, which is wet. I've stood with a shovel
         in my hand. I've spaded the eaten bird over the fence
           into the unclaimed clover. I've the distinct feeling
          I've gotten off with murder. I gather the terms and dash
           a line into the world: *Nothing sidles in the summer....*
It has a sheen, a tricky shine, and wants to rhyme despite me.

44

DEAR BUDAPEST

You kept us vigilant, Budapest,
despite the fact we missed most mornings,
but the bedroom talk mattered
as the sun hung unabashed in windows
as if never complicit in oppression,
as if canonizing the iron roofs
of stripped arsenals would implicate
the energy and tyranny of warmth.
A bright fog fell under the heat. Bullet
-holes in the buildings breathed.
I swallowed a little wine to wake up.
Named the children who'd been
again, weighed them against my age
again, wrote a note about pilfering.

We rechecked the weather to guess
how it would lie to us. The Danube
never looked as cold as it must be, or
as fast, as it advanced my disdain
for frontiersmen and breathed nitrogen
out of the knees of women tethered
to executed men to ration shot. Soon
I'd drink the grapes it irrigated, be drunk
with the woman I love, forget the seasons
of ruin and water's seemingly slow deliverance
wearing all history down to aphorism.
I kissed her twice on each lifted cheek
knowing tomorrow I'd feel the same
beneath similar architecture on a new river.

From the crown of Margaret's Bridge
the Parliament's vanities echoed
rippling light over the Danube's many hips.
I don't have to change, but I will
eat less salt if it means more days of her
before me like a photograph, quiet

above genuflecting gravestones. We stayed
silent, letting affection talk with the murders
while remaining—however crestfallen—
moonstruck. When the bridgeless rivers
of thermal springs soothed my vigil mind,
I did my best to remember the dead.
And when I felt her sulfur-softened body
I knew I'd lost any urge I'd ever have to kill.

FABLE FOR THE CHILD

The child likes the bells that ring out around the house:
fingers on the spathiphyllum, fingers tapping marginata
browning in the shade. Build a hedge around the flora:
let her touch the dying laurel: for all she wrecks she gives
a just reward. Compass her about the little fox of sun
whose presence or absence ruins the borrowed yard.
That red fox is a gray fox in mist and distance. The mist
is lifted off the fox or the red fox has lifted the mist
from off its hackles. The red fox lifts mist from off
the matted patterns in the grass. The patter of darkdeer
was why the child danced, not this mange and gunk
in their eyes, betrayed by the lately lifted mist. The red fox
is golden, resplendent in itself. Parents leave their houses.
The golden pothos chimes: the child dances in the brightness.

ESCHATOLOGY

My irrational fear of bees
                    Is my last relation to god
I turn to sprint and turn
                    I turn but do I really turn
Immaculate and panting
                    I give up a turn There are
Days when I cannot even   Look up I can't
                    See the sun Looking back
I will tell you I'm afraid   I can't hold memory
                    I'm dead and it wasn't
A bee but it was the hand   Which stung I never knew
                    I never held like practical
Flowers papered properly   To mitigate the thorns
                    A hive over water is a voice
Not a murderous colony   I turn more towards
                    The water taken by a voice
It was not the water-voice
                    It was not a righteous bee
No it was the hand I had
                    Never knew I could have
Just voiced I want to hold

One can't will that
nothing ring,
no one call.
No one will call
except with news
about how she did it,
where she's going
and how: general
or behavioral, unwilling
or unconscious
or dead this go.

This go I finished
my drink first and,
no one will doubt,
had a second.
Afterall, fentanyl
fights the naloxone,
stays in the system so
no one will speak
for hours.
No one can.

This must be the place.
Thy will be done
on earth.
This must be it.

Admittance is easy.
I give up all
my possessions.
I give in to being
wanded down
to me and quiet.

Through the secured doors
of the psych ward,
blank, breathable, one
sinks through the drift
of bodies,
sinks through the drift
of wire-hatched glass
knowing
admission (hers or mine,
there's no difference)
will be as trying as finding
the courage to change
the things we can,
our uses and abuses.

Hi. She drifts
in and out,
nodding off and on
along to nothing somewhere.
Where is the music
coming from, the laughter
and labored breath?

Her hands *can* still.
Her eyes.
Her eyes
slowly falling into sight
look through me. Hi.

I feel no being.
I feel my kiss
brought to her
just temple
in endless
endless
assent.

THE ANTHOLOGISTS

You are roiling in the newest star,
a constant measure of the law
of fading. Your fissure in the night
arpeggiates the ocean and sways the suzerain moon
to give the sheet over to your bright tone.
This is jurisdiction. This being on the water's body
as a winking beacon of the heartless light,
an orbed prayer housed in the manner, handless hands,
and endless air of what you are.

That is you. It is yours. You're celeste and citadel.
Your harp and chapel. Palm frond, sea grape, beach plant,
dolphin, shark fin, marlin, they are all descants
in your work's brimmed compendium.
So I will be an old man beside our sister and her sons
curating your composition until I am my own coda's hymn:
This is him. This is him. The fluid crane. The warm pooled waters.
The wind on a dug in bottle's bore, its bassy tone, and the bottle.
Her sons, with sand in their hands saying, This is uncle. This is uncle.

ANTIGONE

When stood in the wheat
of my father's boyhood,
jays hushed a dripping
in my brain. That, then,
was the fleece of heaven.
Now, considering the state
is lent to wind, nylon, heat,
I taste a corroded bronze.
All my time is lustered with violence, but I've been just in scandal.
& loved too well to believe my death won't be sad, wolfish, vanilla.
I'll reject all polity politely & hew that thinking from my hardship.
I'll bask here with my language, open, wasting in your illiterate sun.

PERIPÀTÊTE

      ,minute   ,dissolved   ,the world goes on
aliment
      .No pleasure warmth   .The mouth ,hid
there in the trees ,the tip-top and incommensurable omen saying

I'm headed for mine own   mine .She says a star was my
infancy
      ,or coal ,Or whatever   ,she says .She says ,Prove I'm good
.I have to ,she knows ,not do that ,not cinch the dark with light

.We talk like two criminals   ,having been them once
or twice
      .You know ,I don't say ,when this occurrence has burned
,I will near gratitude and go absolutely and with confidence to awe

.She says ,Prove I'm good   ,and I dissolve in
minutes
      .I can do it ,you know .Easily .That's not
what this is .I'm biding my time .One day ,she'll self-estimate

and we will walk ,minute ,dis   solving out of each other's heads
and lives
      .No pleasure .No loss .The past ,dissolved .We'll walk
through no clearing ,with little clarity ,head to head ,in the trees

VISITATION

You have died
twice now
with nails of varying lengths
like plumb lines into travesty.
You don't need to be
planning that.
Don't do it.
Not so swiftly. Not
at all.
    Shift
this whole belonging drama
to mean I belong to you.
You're not mine.
But I'll keep you
from surface and that depth,
from all space and inner
time, if you wish, if you just
stand there, your humming
pinging off the empty
light.
    Do right,
not swift, and even through
wire-hatched glass
you'll feel our heat
compound and hum.

SÉANCE

I'm godless in the way Spring is not Summer
and so I say it's in your name I turn to birds.
But the birds turn out to be small gods. I turn
Ezekiel down: I bird the bible.   Forgive me
this imagination, which saw you dead
before you died. Below, a woman raises her arm
across an oblivious chest at the crosswalk,
stopping her interlocutor from a sure death,
no caesura in her nocturnal spiel. That's how
I go on knowing you, endlessly casually
as I consider the names of my eventual children
who will carry the censer of our disposition
through aisles of unease before settling in the pews
of these genetics that wait like gracious Satan.
Why censer? What pew? Wherefore Satan?
It's you who's saved me from the most damage,
not god. Can I do things in your name? Yes.
I say your name and I do them.   Brennan,
knife through an orange.   O   Brennan,   answer
the phone.   I can't
feel myself now that we   share
every room. I'm running masking tape down   each horizon
                                                                      —

                          O   Brennan,   stay on your side.

CONTACTS

I like knowing when she will call.
The anxiety of three past any minute now
keeps me flustered in a precious way.
I consider the lighting in a corner
I've never cared for, megaliths,
marine mammals, the half bottle of wine,
and why I let anyone talk me out of drink
before noon. Left with little else
to ease the waiting, my thinking
whisks up each stairwell between us
until her image lies on every landing,
a new bruise blushing on her stiff neck.
I peruse black caskets with satin linings
and cremation urns: pewter or porcelain?

My father's first gift to me was porcelain.
It has not crazed, yet my mother's changed
and my brother's dead. Like this I'm pitched
to the stone fragility of fairness, avoiding
vulnerability's consequence with a thumb
hovering above a name in my list of contacts.
I come to trust she just stopped in the good heat
to look up the name of a misflung flower,
one blue tussle in a tumult of dandelion.
So I say a fast, bashful devotion to my empress
plum and eat. In the nectar's palace
I think of bees' trajectories, flown arcs
of resolute gatherers, heliotropes, sextons,
seed in the wind, and the ocean's bend. Then

I find I like our dog is dying. Something vicious
because tender knows the middle-aged shepherd
regrets letting Brennan go ahead of her
that night he thought of our mother, shot heroin,
got into Child's Pose, and focused on his last breath.
The shepherd's ears perk up to bursts of air

like every wind was god and worth going to.
I know I'm mostly unneeded, but I want to say
I have given unto them. So I lift the dog's jowls
and let her nibble down to the mauve stone
of my half-eaten plum. Suddenly I feel sought,
sacred, and a little guilty that I can't remember
what I promised her when she arrives,
if it was material, or a real change in me.

NOTES

"Opium and Ambergris"
Hunky Dory is David Bowie's fourth studio album. The italicized text is from the second track, "Oh! You Pretty Things."

The epigraph to Part I is taken from the "It Must Give Pleasure" section of Wallace Stevens's *Notes toward a Supreme Fiction.*

"Mementos"
Phenobarbital is an addictive sedative used for epilepsy and alcohol withdrawal. My maternal grandmother and grandfather died from complications with epilepsy and alcoholism, respectively. Section three of the poem references my brother's traumatic brain injury, which he suffered in 2010 while snowboarding in the backcountry of the Sierra Nevadas in Lake Tahoe. He was comatose and on life support for weeks. Brennan snowboarded for the first time after his injury nine months later on December 7, my birthday. On December 7, 1997, my mother's brother John-Michael died from AIDS contracted from shooting heroin. Brennan died of a heroin overdose on March 2, 2013.

"Involuntary Commitment #3"
The structure is based on the "333" grounding technique, which redirects attention from intense anxiety or panic to the present moment by shifting focus to three particulars of sight, sound, and touch. "My twelve meridians" refers to a system in acupuncture, which is my mother's profession. The meridians are the transport system for the body's qi, or vital energy, which are manipulated by needles and, sometimes, electrical stimulation.

"Visitation"
The epigraph is from Czesław Miłosz's "Dedication," which asks: "What is poetry that does not save / Nations or people?" and answers: "A connivance with official lies, / A song of drunkards whose throats will be cut in a moment." The reference to Spinoza refers to a letter of his in which he writes: "I believe that a triangle, if it could speak, would likewise say that God is eminently triangular. . . . In this way each would ascribe to God its own attributes, assuming itself to be like God."

"Mare Liberum"
Literally, "free sea." The UN Convention of the Law of the Sea recognizes sovereign states' rights to exclusive economic zones, which gives them control over the ocean, its contents, and its resources from their coastline to 200 nautical miles into the water. The quotations are from Nietzsche's *The Gay*

Science: "Beside you is the ocean: to be sure, it does not always roar, and at times it lies spread out like silk and gold and reveries of graciousness. But hours will come when you will realize that it is infinite and that there is nothing more awesome than infinity."

"Intrusive Thoughts"

The phrase "moral Seneca" is from Dante's *Inferno,* canto 4 (Limbo), where the "sin" for virtuous pagans was existing before Christ. Seneca is then a suicide saved from outright damnation. "Agenbite of inwit" (again-biting of inner wit; i.e., remorse of conscience) and "Yet here's" (*Macbeth,* 5.1.33) are references to James Joyce's *Ulysses:* "Speaking to me. They wash and tub and scrub. Agenbite of inwit. Conscience. Yet here's a spot." "Agenbite of inwit" is repeated several times in *Ulysses* but comes to its culmination toward the end of the novel as Stephen thinks of his sister's suffering: "She is drowning. Agenbite. Save her. . . . Agenbite of inwit. Inwit's agenbite."

"embodiment"

This was written in India's Thar Desert the morning after my mother and I spread some of Brennan's ashes. The fox was there.

"A Hand's Breadth"

"Psycho Suite" is a piece from Hitchcock's *Psycho* composed by Bernard Herrmann. "The Imperial March" is Darth Vader's theme music in *Star Wars: The Empire Strikes Back,* composed by John Williams. The hurricane is Hurricane Andrew.

"Saturn in Sagittarius"

This poem was written while the planet Saturn was in the constellation Sagittarius. Francisco Goya's *Saturn Devouring His Son* was an inspiration for the poem. Mermaid purse is a colloquialism for the case that surrounds the fertilized eggs of many sharks.

"The Chef and the Wren"

This poem is for my father. "Hand of fire" is in reference to Hart Crane's *The Bridge.* The final lines are riffing on Wallac Stevens's "Of Mere Being": "The palm at the end of the mind, / Beyond the last thought, rises / In the bronze decor, // A gold-feathered bird / Sings in the palm, without human meaning, / Without human feeling, a foreign song."

"Truce"

This poem contains a slight variation on lines from James Merrill's *The Changing Light at Sandover,* which read: "The cloud passed / more quickly than the shade it cast, // Foreshadower of nothing, dearest heart, / But the dim wish of lives to drift apart."

"Swift History"
Ugolino della Gherardesca was accused of treachery after the murder of the Archbishop of Pisa's nephew. He was imprisoned and starved in a jail tower in Pisa with his sons and grandsons, whom he may have eaten to stay alive. His story is recounted in Dante's *Inferno,* canto 33.

The epigraph to Part II is taken from Herman Melville's *Moby-Dick.*

"Apus Apus in Air"
The line "a love overpassed to" is a reference to William Faulkner's *Absalom, Absalom!* His "overpass to love" involves reciprocal acknowledgment and exchange, or the "happy marriage of speaking and hearing." The line "alone on a wide wide sea" is from Samuel Taylor Coleridge's *The Rime of the Ancient Mariner;* "then the Line" is in reference to the "Argument" section of the same poem.

"The Gravity of Grace"
The title and fire metaphor of this poem are in reference to St. Augustine's theory of bodies and love in *Confessions:* "A body gravitates to its proper place by its own weight . . . the fire tends upward, a stone downward. . . . They are not at rest as long as they are disordered, but once brought to order they find their rest. Now, my weight is my love, and wherever I am carried, it is this weight that carries me."

"Involuntary Commitment #6"
This poem takes language from "Anaphora" by Elizabeth Bishop, "This Must Be the Place (Naive Melody)" by Talking Heads, and the "Serenity Prayer" recited in Alcoholics/Narcotics Anonymous meetings.

"The Anthologists"
This poem is for my sister, Caitlin.

"Peripàtête"
"Peripàtête" is a neologism combining "peripatetic" and "tête-à-tête." Walking and talking in circles was one of the only activities my mother would entertain when hospitalized for her depression. The line "I will near gratitude and go absolutely and with confidence to awe" is a variation of lines from John Berryman's "Eleven Addresses to the Lord."